T0061139

What Color Is the Sky?

Trent Johnson

It is the middle of the night.

The sky is black.

It is early in the morning.
The sun is rising.

The sky is orange and yellow.

It is noon.
The sun is high in the sky.

The sky is blue.

It is late in the afternoon.
A storm is coming.

The sky is gray.

The storm is over.
The rain has stopped.

What can you see in the sky now?

A rainbow!